**CONFRONTING THE
AGE-OLD QUESTION:**

WHY ME?

BY: PRECIOUS SIMONÉ

Copyright © 2017 Precious Simoné
All rights reserved.
ISBN: 1981233571
ISBN-13: 978-1981233571

ACKNOWLEDGMENTS

I would like to thank my family, friends, mentors and leaders for their endless support. To my mother, thanks for your tough and unconditional love. Your tough love has strengthened me during the most difficult times. I don't know what I would do without you. To my sisters/brothers, thank you for never judging me and always offering a word of encouragement. To my friends, thanks for always speaking life into me and reassuring me of my purpose and the mandate on my life. To my mentors and my leaders, thank you for your wisdom, counsel, sacrifice, discipline, and prayers. You were instrumental in my journey to wholeness and for that I am thankful. I am forever grateful and wouldn't be the woman I am today without my mother, sisters/brothers, friends, leaders, and mentors. I love you all dearly and cherish everything you are and have added to me in my journey of becoming whole. Thanks for always being there and never giving up on me.

~Precious Simone

FOREWORD

Confronting the Age-Old Question: Why Me? is a book you can't afford to not have in your library. The book is relevant to our positions in life, our identities, our hopes, and our dreams. That question – Why Me? – finds its way into our thoughts, and sometimes, it's difficult to know the answer. To do so, one has to be honest with themselves and take on all that comes with knowing the truth of that answer, once revealed; but if we are being honest, most times, we aren't up to hear or receive that truth.

This book dives into discovering - why me, why you, or why any of us. More than that, it illuminates the power of why not me. Precious has taken time to allow us into one of the very most intimate parts of her life, so that we can all discover why me; so that we can all know why me; so that we can all see the purpose of why me. She speaks from not only her own experience, but from the experiences of those she's encountered and encouraged firsthand, who have dealt with the questions in their mind and in their hearts, who have begun to find their place in life again. The transparency that she affords us is both refreshing and necessary; she is so relatable. Not only does she write about the pain she has endured on her journey from brokenness to wholeness, she talks about the purpose of it all.

From this book, you will learn how to push past the insecurities, the fears, the anger, the disappointments, and the questions; and you'll learn how to stand in the truth of what is and what will be. If you allow it, I know the heart of the author will reach you through the word of this book, and meet you right where you are. It doesn't matter if you are lost, confused, hurt, broken, bitter, or empty, you will be strengthened and encouraged in the pages ahead. Congratulations to you for wanting wholeness and seeking after it. Let this book be your guide while on your personal journey to wholeness.

Forward by:
Darlyshia A. Menzie, author of the book *At The End of Me*

INTRODUCTION

If you've been living for some time, you've probably asked yourself the age-old question, why me? You've often pondered the thoughts, "I'm a good person;" "I treat others with respect;" "I am giving;" "I'm loving;" "I'm caring;" and "I'm loyal." The list goes on. But, why me? You've asked yourself and others what did I do to deserve this? What did I do to end up in this situation? Why am I, of all people, going through this? Again, why me?

I understand this question all too well. I found myself in a position in life where the only question I could ask myself for 5 years was why, me? My thoughts were; I'm a good woman, so why me? I'm there when others need me, so why me? I'm a giver, so why me? I'm patient and thoughtful, so why me? Even deeper, I'm educated; so why me? I'm good looking, so why me? I'm well put together, so why me? I've waited, so why me?

This question plagued my mind for 5 years because I couldn't conceptualize why I was going through the things I was going through. I was at a place in my life that the pain was so unbearable and if I didn't get the answer to that question, I wasn't sure I was going to make it.

So, when did this question arise? I'm glad you asked. Allow me to take you on a quick journey of my life so that you can see how this question came about and the steps I took to overcome.

CONTENTS

Acknowledgments
Foreword
Introduction

It All Started When	1
The Turning Point	4
Why Me?	6
Desperate for Change	13
The Audacity of Singleness	19
Choose Your Audience Carefully	28
Transforming from Within	34
Everything Happens for a Reason	38
From Pity to Purpose	47
Questions to Ponder	60
Share Your Story	61

IT ALL STARTED WHEN

I was at a conference in December of 2009 and received the following word. "Precious, God is going to use you. He has a plan for your life. He has a mate that he has handpicked for you. May he hold you in the palm of his hands until he sends that mate to you. You two are going to be mighty and powerful in the things of God."

Husband! Yes, that's true, my exact thoughts were husband! Believe it or not, that was the main thing that stood out to me from that prophetic word. And if you'll be honest with yourself, there are many times we as men and women receive a word and there is one thing from that word that stood out to us the most. In my case, it was hearing the word husband.

I was so happy about that word I had to share it with everyone. "Y'all, God has a husband for me! He has handpicked him for me!" I was so excited to hear these words that I didn't know what would come with it. I was 23 years old when I received that word. In my zest for life and zeal for the things of God, I graduated from college, moved back to my hometown with a word in my heart and a desire to see it fulfilled.

Two months post undergrad, I met a young man who I KNEW had to be the one. I was on fire for God. He was on fire for God. I attended church and so did he. He was chivalrous, handsome, well-spoken and he had a sense of humor. Surely, this must be my husband, ya'll. This young man and I started spending time together. We prayed, ministered and witnessed to others together. We had mutual interest, aspirations and goals. You couldn't tell me nothing. I was sold. The package was mine. He must be the one! The connection was so strong, and I thought to myself, I wish somebody would tell me otherwise.

So, guess what happened? We began a courtship together and I was extremely happy. On top of that, I was working at a job I loved; I had just purchased my first vehicle; and again, this guy may be my husband. What else could go right? I fell in love with us quickly. I enjoyed spending time with him and building memories. We were inseparable. We spent so much time together that one day I looked up and he popped the question, "will you marry me?" Whaaaaat?! There is no way! Is this really happening? Could this really be? In my excitement I happily said, "yes!" I was the happiest woman on planet earth.

We paid a trip to my college town to get counsel from a pastor of mine. When he met with us, he told us that marriages don't fail, people fail. He asked us if we loved each other, and we both happily stated yes. He told us that he was going to do his best to talk us out of getting married because marriage was serious business, and if he can talk us out of it, then marriage was not for us. Welp, we walked away from that session very much in love and still desired to marry one another. So, what happened next? Hold on, I'm getting there. Relax, it's a journey.

THE TURNING POINT

I now pronounce you husband and wife! Yay! You guessed right. We got married in January of 2012. And once again, I was the happiest girl on planet earth. We'd finally moved in together and ready to jump-start our lives as one. Everything was going well. We had the same level of cleanliness and orderly mannerisms. We both unplugged household appliances after each use and didn't like all the lights on in the house at one time. This was a win! You could only imagine that I was leaping for joy on the inside. Again, we were inseparable; the Dynamic Duo if you ask me, or anyone else for that matter. We were prayer warriors. Both of us had a love in our heart for people and we were both family-oriented. I felt so blessed to be a wife. I always desired to be a wife someday, so for this to happen to me meant everything and so much more.

Seven months into the marriage, tragedy struck on both sides of the family. Instead of the tragedies bringing us closer together, they were pulling us further apart. Even in the midst of having strong faith and being like-minded believers, it seemed impossible to hold on to one another. Communication became a struggle. Interacting, spending time with one another and the concept of love was being quickly redefined. So, being the woman that I am, I immediately thought to troubleshoot. I thought to myself, "Fix whatever is going on! Pray, read, fast, get wise counsel, talk to trusted friends, seek wisdom, seek advice!" "Father, HELP!" I remember uttering the words, "Whatever it takes, we are GOING to get through this."

WHY ME?

Things began to get better. Well, in my opinion they did. The optimist in me saw that communication was getting better. We were interacting, we crossed a small threshold and started to spend time together. One evening, we had a marital bible study. For those of you who don't know what that means - it's a modern-day term for argument; a heated discussion. We weren't seeing eye to eye on a situation, and since I don't like to leave an argument with unresolved feelings, I aggressively expressed my unhappiness with how we were handling the situation. I remember walking away from that moment receiving a message that said,

"I don't like the way that you communicate and in my heart and in my mind, I don't desire to be in this relationship."

What? Are you kidding me? This is a silly joke? This has to be a game! I gathered up some internal strength and thought, "Boy please! You ain't going nowhere. We said to death do we part and we ain't dead yet, so yeah, you stuck with me. We said for better or for worse, so if this is worse, then you gone have to stick it out.

Maybe he intended this message to be sent to someone else. Surely this message wouldn't be sent to someone like me!"

Remember y'all, I'm loving. I'm caring. I'm loyal and faithful. I'm supportive. I'm thoughtful. I'm trustworthy. I'm beautiful. I'm a great wife. I'm educated. Dang, WHY ME??

At that very moment is when I was first confronted with the question – WHY ME? I thought to myself, "This can't be. What did I say that was that bad? What did I do? Did I really just get that message? What do I do now?".

I left the house and went for a walk in the park trying to process that message. I mean, I just couldn't make sense of it - I cried; I rebuked the devil; I even laughed...that's weird ain't it? I cried some more. Called out spirits and anything trying to destroy my marriage and my home. I jogged. Yeah, we've all been there. I had no control over my emotions y'all. I was in disarray. I ended up calling one of my prayer partners at the time and shared with her what was going on. My goal at this point is to get my husband and I back to normal, by any means necessary. With that in mind, she prayed with me and I felt better, but it didn't take away from the shock of it all.

I returned home from my walk in the park and the lights were off. He was in bed, and hesitantly, I crawled in too. Internally, I was shattered, so at this point I don't know if holding him is the right move to make. I'm a quality time and a physical touch kind of girl so you can imagine the struggle I was having with myself. The evening concluded with me in a fetal position holding on tightly to my pillow, while tears were streaming down my face. Up until this point, if we ever had an argument or a disagreement, we would go our separate ways, process it and come back to figure it out. I didn't know how to come back home and be face-to-face with the one who'd just hurt me without any resolve. This was a real struggle.

The next day I told myself, "Girl, get over yourself! You are stronger than this! You are not going to allow those words to break you. He doesn't mean what he said. We just weren't seeing eye-to-eye and he said something he didn't mean." Internally, I told myself to proceed as usual. Stay a good wife. Clean, cook, love on him and act like those words were never said. So that's what I did. I started serving my husband and striving to please him in the flesh. I did everything in my power to prove to him that he still wanted and desired us. He loved certain snacks, so I would go out and buy his favorite snacks and leave love baskets around the house to show him that I loved him and was going to do whatever it took to save us. I left cards with messages and tried to change the way I communicated since he mentioned that was something that he didn't like.

Little did I know, none of that was working. Earlier you heard me say I proceeded as if that statement never happened. Yeah, never do that. Even though I didn't like to leave arguments unresolved, this was a sensitive matter. This is not a war with words; what I'm dealing with is matters of the heart. The man that I love so much doesn't want the relationship anymore, and now, I am serving him in a broken state.

So, guess what happens to Precious? Precious is growing insecure. She is second guessing herself. She is wondering why her husband doesn't want her anymore. The atmosphere at home was very cold and there was a great distance between us. Y'all, I never shared with him how his message made me feel. I didn't know how to address it. I didn't know where to start. I didn't know what to say. So, I walked on eggshells because I didn't want anything else to add to his reason for not wanting us anymore. On a normal day, I would be bubbly and energetic but that all changed and I began to change my personality.

This went on for several months. Lack of communication, no quality time and no connection. We had turned into complete strangers. When I did communicate with him, I was very short with him and barely made eye contact. I was still trying my best to be a good wife, but once again, I was broken. Those words impacted me more than which I ever gave them credit.

I'm cleaning - broken. I'm cooking - broken. Serving - broken. I am loving him - broken. I was waiting on him to tell me that he didn't mean what he said - just broken. I was waiting to hear, "Baby, I'm sorry. I must have been crazy and out of my mind. I don't know what came over me. I love you and want to be with you."

I was desperate for some type of affirmation and validation that THIS is still where he wanted to be. I got NOTHING. Not a word, not a look, not a gesture, not even a hint. I got NOTHING! What was I supposed to do at that point? I was battling with him not wanting me. I never realized how much it hurt me for someone to not want me and I learned at that moment that I was afraid of rejection. The idea of someone not wanting me scared me to death. I had never experienced that feeling, EVER, and I would never wish that on anyone. I also learned that I didn't handle disappointments well and I didn't respond well to being let down. As bold and outgoing of a person that I am, when I am wounded emotionally, I don't handle that well. And to be honest, I didn't know that until I was hit with this situation.

When I encountered people who loved us, they would ask me how we were doing, and out of fear, shame, and embarrassment, I masked what we were going through. I would say "We are doing well. Keep praying for us." They didn't know that deep down inside, I was dying emotionally. I would ride past places where we spent time together and just cry. On top of that, playing R&B songs that spoke about love didn't make it easier.

#AMOMENTWITHPRECIOUS

Y'all, I don't know WHY we put ourselves in more pain listening to songs about what we are going through. I don't know if we enjoy seeing ourselves cry or what, but for some reason that's what we resort to when we are hurting.

DESPERATE FOR CHANGE

The times I rode in the car alone, driving past places that made me think of the times we had together, caused something to rise in me that made me want to fight hard for my marriage. Not that I wasn't fighting before, but it was something about those memories that made me believe that we could have that again. So what did I do? In my desperation for my relationship, I called and text, begged and pleaded, and sent pictures of us to him. I thought, truly this will make him want us more or at least want US again. I figured, if I'm touched by these memories, then surely, he will be touched as well. I sent long messages and emails reminding him of the good times we had together. I was quoting songs in my messages. I know you're nodding your head right now because you can relate. One time, I sent him some of the lyrics to Mariah Carey's song, "Don't Forget About Us."

I said, "Remember us at our best. I know it's hard to see us at our best in the current state that we are in, but remember the good times we had. Don't allow these stressful moments to cause you not to see us in the light you originally saw our relationship."

I recall saying, "Remember the word that was given to us. We are going to be powerful together; we have purpose together. Let's not allow the bad times to make us think differently about one another."

~~~~~~

#AMOMENTWITHPRECIOUS

Oftentimes, we allow the bad times to get in the way of how we truly feel about the ones we say we love. We allow difficulties and differences to cloud our vision, and in return, we find ourselves altering our outlook on what we once held to be true.

~~~~~~

I was desperate for a change. I wanted him to know that I remembered what we shared. I remembered how we looked at one another. I know you know what I mean! Don't tell me that I'm the only one that's had moments shared looking into the eyes of the one you love. I figured sharing he and I's experiences with him, sending pictures, sending love notes, and pouring out more love, would change things. Surely, this is touching and reaching him, I thought. Thinking about it, the pain of what happened to us and what I was doing was driving me even more insane. I couldn't stomach not being in a relationship anymore. I didn't like it y'all. I didn't enjoy being alone. How do you bounce back from date nights, going home to someone every night, being able to share the intimate details of your heart, sharing your ambitions and aspirations - to nothing. I felt empty. I felt the void. I could feel the weight of not being with him.

After being married, I didn't want to be single. I didn't like the idea of coming home every day to myself. I was angry inside. I was frustrated. I didn't understand why we just couldn't work it out. I thought, why can't we be together? What is the issue? I had so many questions and not enough answers.

I kept trying, kept sending messages, kept sending pictures.

Then, one day, I finally got a response. So much is going through my mind right now. It's the moment I've been waiting for. After everything that I've been doing, I wonder what he's about to say. How is he about to respond? I was anxiously excited and nervous at the same time. I thought about if I should I open the message or not. I smiled and cried at the same time. I didn't know what to expect. I just wanted to know what was inside this message. So I opened the message and it read…..

"Precious, you and I are not going to be together." "I have no desire to be in a relationship." "Just go on."

So here I go. I started pacing the floor and talking to myself. I thought in my head, I don't want to move on. I don't desire anyone or anything else, BUT YOU, and to be with YOU. Why do I have to let go? Why do I have to move on? I just didn't understand, and to be honest, I didn't want to understand. I thought, surely, we can work this out. We can fix this.

I went into question mode again. "What did I do?" "What do I need to change?" "What's the problem?" "What will make you want it?" "What's wrong with me?" "Why can't we be together?" "What do I need to do to change his mind?" I was desperate. I needed to know what would reach him. I convinced myself again that he didn't mean it. So, I kept moving forward believing that he would eventually come back around and things would get better. I kept this mindset for years. Hoping, believing, and waiting. I felt, surely the time will come and I will pinch myself and this all would all be a horrible dream and it never happened. Welp, that only happens in movies.

Years went by and I continued to feel the pangs of our broken relationship. It wasn't an easy journey. The memories continued to haunt me. Songs reminded me of the heartbreak, and being around mutual friends and family didn't make things better for me. I started to resent the relationship and even regret ever being in the relationship. I asked myself, "Why did you get married? Was it real? Was this a game? Did you guys ever love one another? If he loved you, would he have ever put you through this? Why is this so hard? Should I continue to fight, or should I let go? Do I keep pressing in desperation or do I let it go and walk away?" I was torn and didn't have a clue as to what I should do. Love, shouldn't be this hard.

THE AUDACITY OF SINGLENESS

Suddenly, my close friends began courting and everyone was happy in their relationships, but me. What happened? I thought we were all supposed to be happy together. I was extremely happy for them, but unhappy with my situation because it made me think about the talks we had about the day we would all be married. We would have lady's night and sit up and talk about who was next. Cheesy, huh? Well that's how we rolled together. Don't judge us, LOL!

My trusted friends could see the pain in my eyes. What I love the most about them was that I never had to say a word. They would walk over to me, give me a hug, and I would instantly break down. They didn't have a clue what I was going through, but they could feel it. One friend, in particular, eventually asked and I had to be honest with her. I had to be honest with her and myself because I couldn't keep going on like this. I am broken and in a lot of pain and no one knows this. You may be asking, why are you holding all of this in? Girl, tell somebody, already! Well y'all, I couldn't. Not the girl who got the prophecy over her life about her husband. Are you kidding me!?! That's embarrassing. How can I even begin to tell what I'm going through? How do I share? Who do I tell? What will they think?

I was drowning in shame and all of these emotions were eating me alive.

So, I finally admitted it. I finally confessed to her and myself out loud - I'm DIVORCED! She cried in disbelief. "Precious, No!" "Yes," I said with disappointment. I had to be real. It was time to let it out. I was emotionally constipated. Something has to give and I might as well suck it up and come clean. I never wanted to accept it. I didn't want to use that word…divorce. The thought of it made me sick to my stomach. The reality of being divorced was torturing me.

I would have random crying spells and I really needed emotional healing. I was fighting a losing battle and I couldn't keep this to myself any longer. I needed help! My husband and I needed help at the time, but I'm the one who was taking this situation very hard. I was dying inside. I was unhealthy and had become an emotional wreck. I was in utter turmoil and couldn't hold it together any longer.

I didn't like going out in public anymore because he and I weren't together. I didn't like being invited to events because I was afraid of the question, "where's your husband? Y'all doing okay?" I avoided anything that would draw attention to me, and us not being together, for that matter. When I went to social outings and gatherings, I wouldn't stay long because it was hard for me to have fun without him. On top of that, everyone is having a good time with their woman or their man and I'm not, so this isn't fun for me. I felt I didn't have value or worth anymore because I no longer had "a man." Crazy huh? Well, it's the truth. It seemed at the time that being married added value and losing that made me feel as if I no longer had value. Everyone else had value being married but me.

Family events were extremely difficult to attend and holidays were the worst. It took me 2 years to tell my family that we were divorced. I didn't know how to face them. What will they think of me? What will they say? What will they think of him? How will they handle this news? Where do I start?

After sharing with my family, I received a call from one of my sisters and she said, "Precious, why didn't you come to me and talk to me? I replied, "who picks up the phone and shares that information? I didn't know how to tell anyone and I wasn't happy to be sharing that news." I said, "who goes around happily sharing they are divorced?" Not me.

I was going through it y'all. If I were to be honest, it was hard being around my family, friends, and their relationships because they had and were developing something I once had. I desperately wanted that feeling again.

#AMOMENTWITHPRECIOUS

If you'll be honest with yourself, you've been there before wanting that one person to love you and want you the same way you love and want them.

I remember encountering different guys after the severance of my relationship and they would acknowledge my beauty, share the things they loved about my personality, affirm my value and worth as a woman and express their appreciation for me as a person. Though it was refreshing to hear, sadly, it did nothing for me. I know right! It's unfortunate, but it was true. You would think hearing those words would light me up on the inside, but it didn't. One of those guys could tell that I was still hurting and he said, "Precious, you're not going to be good for anyone if you don't get healed." Sad, huh? Well, that's how broken I was.

Have you ever been in that place? It doesn't matter how much greatness another man or another woman sees in you, you just want that one person to see it. You dress a certain way so they can see you. You start working out and switching up your wardrobe. You say certain things so they can recognize it. Come on now, I know I'm not the only one who has been there. For me, I only wanted to be validated and affirmed by him, so anybody who came after him, though their words were great, it didn't carry as much weight because I wanted those words to only come from him.

I had become so insecure that I felt that if he didn't want me, with everything that I brought to the table, then no other man would want me. Crazy thinking, but you never know the thoughts that will take up space in your mind when you are broken.

I pushed everyone away who showed interest in me out of fear that they too would eventually not want me. I used the famous "it's not you, it's me" line. I was afraid that they would eventually hurt me in the same way that I was previously hurt. I also felt that I would never be able to give someone else the best of me because I felt as though I gave it all in this relationship. My insecurities and fears were getting the best of me.

I remember sharing with a friend that I never wanted to get married again. She said, "Precious, don't say that." I shouted at her and said "Who wants to start over? Who wants to share their secrets with someone else? Who wants to rebuild with someone else? What if they do the same thing?" In my mind, I figured that if I found love and marriage, and this is what it is, then I never want to do this again.

She would say "Precious, let's pray because you are still hurting. You can't allow this one situation to make you feel that this is the reality of all marriages." She had a good point and I knew marriage was a beautiful thing, but, in my brokenness, it was hard to see the beauty of it all.

I went back to questioning, why me? What did I do to deserve this? I hate how this feels! When will the pain end? I was going to church, broken. Great messages would come from the pulpit and I would even receive personal messages about God wanting to heal me, but I still couldn't see past the pain inside.

I would call my mentor and trusted friends and have them pray for us. I joined prayer calls. I would go for walks with my sister and brother and just cry. They would just listen. They didn't know how to help and they didn't know what to say, but they were there. They would give me hugs and tell me everything was going to be okay. I lost my smile. Yes, Precious lost her smile.

#AMOMENTWITHPRECIOUS

May I share that even in the midst of all of that I never slandered his name. I never male bashed or tried to make him look like the bad guy. I didn't go live on social media and expose the things I was dealing with because that's not the place for that. Social media is not that platform for your pain.

CHOOSE YOUR AUDIENCE CAREFULLY: KNOW WHERE TO VENT

I highly caution individuals when taking their pain to social media. I know our emotions get the best of us at times when we are wounded, but taking your pain to social media can cause more damage if you ask me. If I took that approach, it wouldn't have made the situation better; it wouldn't have relieved the pain. It would have been a place to vent and express my inner most feelings, but it would not have gotten me the resolve I was looking for.

My heart was for the both of us to be healed. I knew that if I was hurting this bad, he had to be experiencing some level of hurt as well. I didn't desire to trash his image as a man or sabotage his character. I only wanted to know, why me? I wanted to know how did we get to this place. I wanted to know what was going on in him that got us here. Social media didn't have that answer.

Actually, when I finally opened up to share the things I was going through, I would speak life back into him. I would speak life back into us. At the end of the day, what we were going through didn't change the fact that he was a great man with a call on his life.

It didn't change the qualities that I loved about him as a man. He was in his personal storm, as well as I. But this was about me! I needed healing! I needed to know how to get through this.

One day, I called my mentor and shared some things that were on my heart and she talked to me about forgiveness. She said, "Precious, you have to forgive him for this pain you feel and you have to quit holding him hostage. You have to forgive yourself and you have to forgive him. Forgiveness will happen in its own time, but God needs for you to forgive." She said, "it doesn't excuse what happened and we don't know why it happened, but you have to let go and come out of this pain."

That was easier said than done. How do I forgive someone who has broken my heart? I mean, I know what the Bible says about forgiveness, but I really needed practical tools on how to forgive. Through this process, I learned that I was good at holding grudges, and boy was I good at it too, but I also had a problem with letting hurt go. I said to myself, "I'm a believer, why can't I lay down the hurt? This should be easy! Quote the Bible, right." Well, I did quote the Bible, but I was quoting it in a broken and unforgiving state. So the depths of what I was quoting had no weight because of the condition of my heart.

Ya'll, this situation made me so angry. I grew bitter inside and I started questioning God's plan for my life. I had so many unanswered questions. I didn't understand WHY US or WHY ME? But, one thing I knew for sure is that I wanted to be healed. I didn't want to stay in this place of pain. I didn't want to keep crying. I didn't want my heart to stay in this condition. I knew that I didn't want to look up and be in the same place in 10 years, stuck, knowing that I had already asked "why me" for 5 of those years. I didn't want to look up and still be asking the same questions - why me?

After all of my striving, I finally got to a place where I had to give him, me, and us to God. You would think that would have been my first thought, right? Well, sorry to disappoint you, but even spirit-filled believers who love God struggle with running to Him in the midst of pain.

I was encouraged by others to run to the Father; trust the Father. "He will take care of you," they said. All of that was great and I will never discredit it, but how does one run to the Father when they never had a father to even know what that looks like. I was stuck. I wanted healing, but I was stuck. I didn't have a natural father to whom I could run. My father passed away when I was 5 years old, so I don't know what it means to crawl in the Father's lap. I didn't know what it meant to run to the Father.

So I tried it. I put my Bible down in front of me, I got down on my knees, went into prayer and started asking the Father for forgiveness and asking him to heal my heart and asked him to heal my husband. I spoke life over him. I began to speak life over his work and everything that pertained to him. I prayed to the Father to help me to learn how to forgive him and I prayed that I wouldn't hold him hostage to this pain anymore.

#AMOMENTWITHPRECIOUS

I dare you to forgive. Release others when they hurt you. Holding on will get you nowhere. When you make the conscious decision to forgive, the prisoner that is really set free is you.

All of a sudden, I had a deeper desire and longing to cover him and desired the best for him, even if it wasn't with me. I had never been in that place before or prayed anything like that, so I even shocked myself praying that prayer. It was an inner relief.

I got up from off my knees and picked up my Bible. I was drawn to the book of Psalms and turned to Psalm 68:5a. The verse read, "He is a father to the fatherless." That comforted me and I remember feeling a huge release. I've always heard people say in church that He [God] is a mother to the motherless and a father to the fatherless, but I never experienced the true essence of what that meant until that day when I had to deal with feelings of how to run to Him as Father. I also remember reading a verse that said, "never will I leave you and never will I forsake you." It was something about these verses that stuck with me throughout this journey that gave me the strength to get back up.

TRANSFORMING FROM WITHIN

After this moment, I started to feel different. I noticed that my heart was feeling better. I noticed when I interacted with friends and family, I was full of joy. I began to smile again and feel good about where I was in life and began to realize why I had gone through the things I had gone through.

I began to have fresh perspective. I wasn't mad anymore. The anger subsided. When I shared my story, I spoke about it from a place of joy, instead of pain and shame. I spoke about it as if I was supposed to go through it. I was thankful for what I had gone through and what it had taught me about myself as a woman. I didn't cry when I shared the story anymore. There was a time that I couldn't talk about the divorce without crying and I was no longer in that place. I thought, someone pinch me. Is this really real? Is the pain really gone?

I would see him out at an engagement and I didn't have any bitterness or anger in my heart. Whaaat?...No ill feelings? I was so confused! I was happy, but I was confused. We were cordial and would even laugh with one another. There was a time during this journey that I couldn't be around him without crying or feeling the weight of disappointment of what we had gone through. That was no longer our reality. I was able to have decent conversations with him and I felt great on the inside. I would leave his presence and not be hurting and holding on to anything from the past. I knew I still cared, but I wasn't in a desperate state of longing for he and I to be together.

I would often think to myself, wow! How did I get here? Where did that come from? What was happening to me?! Well I shared with you earlier, I desired to be healed. I didn't want the pain strangling the cords of my heart anymore. I was becoming whole. I wasn't broken anymore. See, when you are broken you are in a damaged state. You are emotionally fragile and your heart is shattered. On the contrary, when you are whole, you are not in a broken or damaged state. You are in a state of peace and everything is harmonious. You're well in your body, mind, soul and spirit. Wholeness is a state of liberty, and fulfillment. I was truly starting to experience what it meant to be fulfilled.

Two of my friends approached me one day and said "Precious, we should start a group to encourage and support one another."

They said, "I know a group of ladies who are going through some trying times and could use some support, encouragement, and love." I was excited about that because I loved helping others and was committed to empowering people.

We started meeting once a week and it was the best time ever. We would pray and encourage one another. They shared stories about their past and present experiences and we started to strengthen one another. I looked up and realized that the more I met with the ladies, allowing them to pour into me and vice versa, I was getting better emotionally. I was busy helping others in their journey that I totally forgot that I went through my situation. I finally got to a place in which I was ready to talk about my insecurities, my battle with rejection, shame and embarrassment, and my battle with being a divorced woman. When I came to share my story, the ladies from the group were shocked and in disbelief because they never thought that I would struggle with something like that.

I took the time to share with them the right things to do in their relationships and how to have healthy marriages and healthy relationships. I thought to myself, "Precious, who are you to be sharing how to have a healthy marriage or relationship when you are divorced?" I had to keep in mind that everything about my relationship wasn't bad. I knew what it took to be a good wife and I also came to know the mistakes I made in lashing out and not opening up when I felt hurt. I held on to the good memories, which was the reason why I fought for us so long, and I didn't want to let us go because of those memories.

Men and women would reach out regarding their spouses and I would encourage them to respect and love their spouses. I encouraged them to forgive and to let go of the pain of the past. I encouraged them to be responsible for their roles in their relationships and not focus on trying to change their spouse or significant other.

EVERYTHING HAPPENS FOR A REASON

I recall a time when one of my best friends reached out to me to share that a friend of hers was going through a rough time in her marriage and she felt that my story would benefit her. She told her friend that she wanted her to meet up with someone who may be able to encourage her in her situation. Her friend and I had previous encounters with one another, however she never revealed to her that I was the woman with whom she was coming to speak. They came over to my house that night and the young lady was in complete shock to learn that I was the woman who had the story to share. She uttered, "NO WAY!!"

~~~~~~

#AMOMENTWITHPRECIOUS

Be a blessing and share your story! It's important to get whole and get to a healthy state because you never how your story may benefit the next person.

~~~~~~

She couldn't believe it was me. She said, "I wouldn't have ever known you went through a divorce." When she met me, I was in a healthy state. She didn't meet me broken, so she wouldn't have ever known. If she had met me broken, I wouldn't have ever gotten the opportunity to connect with her that evening.

The young lady shared her story and I was humbled to be able to pour life back into her. I shared my story with her and encouraged her in the right things to do as a wife and the things to avoid. I learned after that session that she and her husband's relationship was restored and they were doing much better.

#AMOMENTWITHPRECIOUS

When offering wisdom or advice to a man or a woman regarding their relationship, remember you're for the relationship. Oftentimes, we become team wife or team husband, or team her or team him, when in fact you should be team marriage/relationship. You are for THEM!

Another friend of mine reached out and asked that I share my story with a young man that they knew very well. I met the young man and he shared his story about the things that he was dealing with concerning his wife, and I was able to provide insight on what she may be feeling and why she was acting the way that she was acting. He acknowledged some things that he needed to change. He acknowledged the need to forgive her, and I learned shortly after that his marriage was restored and he and his wife were doing very well.

So my pain became my purpose and I was dedicated to the cause of not seeing men and women go through the things that I went through. I encouraged them to communicate openly when they are hurting because I knew I didn't do that. I encouraged them to take time for each other because neglect could leave a damaging mark on their relationship. Marriages were being healed, relationships were being restored, hearts were being mended and individuals were getting stronger in their unions. It was a joy to be a part of such transformation. The message in my heart was not just for the married or the divorced. At that time, it seemed those were the people who were crossing my path. The message was also for the ones battling rejection, shame, guilt and embarrassment. It was for the ones struggling to love themselves, forgive and know their worth. It was for the ones who plowed through loneliness and didn't know how to forgive.

But, guess what?? Discouragement crept upon me suddenly. I began to wonder - how is it that I've been believing with people, praying with them, and pouring into them, and it's happening for them, but it's not happening for me? Why me?

#AMOMENTWITHPRECIOUS

When you say you believe and commit to something, don't ever think that you won't be tested.

Why did everyone's situation work out but mine? My inner voice would say, "But you believe and trust God, Precious. You are strong! You have faith. You're not supposed to feel this way." I know right, my thoughts exactly. All of the above are true, but that doesn't mean I didn't get to a place in my finite being where I wondered how the tips I shared with others worked for them, but not for me.

You see to actually know just how strong you are, your strength must be challenged. We can make our mouths say anything to convince others, and even ourselves, but the proof is in the pudding. When good times or adversity strike, do we say "WHY ME or WHY NOT ME"? We have been given the privilege, now are we strong enough to shoulder the responsibility? The resounding reply should be YES! YES! YES!

This led me to confront the question: WHY ME?

~~~~~~

#AMOMENTWITHPRECIOUS

We are a temporary part of the whole scheme of this thing called life.

~~~~~~

FROM PITY TO PURPOSE

Why Me? I'll tell you why...

God knew I could handle it. He knew I would run to him eventually! He knew I needed him to help me through it. Many would have given me negative advice and would have shared their famous, "if I were you" line and possibly led me into deeper hurt.

Be mindful of the people who come into your life and say, "if I were you." Well, you're not that person nor are you in their situation and you don't know how you'd respond if given that same situation or walking in those same shoes.

Why Me?
I had to go through this to learn how the Father loves. I had to learn what unconditional love looked like; not only that, but how it ought to be lived out.

Why Me?
God knew there would be some men and women out there who would experience battle with rejection, heartache, pain and insecurities. He knew they would need to know how to overcome.

Why Me?

I needed character development and my heart needed to be dealt with. I needed to be healed and I needed a cleanse. Sometimes, everything that's happening to you isn't bad.

You've heard the age-old saying, No Pain, No Gain. Well, I have to liken that saying to the concept of a battery. A battery has a negative and a positive charge. We have the positives of life and we have the negatives, but they both benefit us. Same way with the battery, the negative charge isn't better for the battery and neither is the positive charge better, but they both benefit the life of the battery. We have to learn in life how the negatives benefit us. They make us stronger, wiser, and better.

We've also heard the saying, Hurt People, Hurt People. I like to say hurting people hurt people. When you've been hurt, typically you don't want to feel that pain again so you'll do your best to avoid it and prevent others from feeling that same pain. But if you're hurting, that's a present state of being. So hurting people hurt people because they are still feeling the pain. They are still feeling the sting of what hurt them. They are in a present state of sadness so they are more than likely going to hurt others because they intentionally want others to feel the weight of their pain. It's common knowledge that, Misery Loves Company. Well, for the hurting, company is anyone that will share in their misery. You don't have to agree, it's just my perspective.

Today, I am thankful for this journey. I am glad that I went through this process of becoming whole. Even the heartache was necessary, and learning how to forgive was beneficial for me. I am not ashamed or afraid to admit that it was important for me to embrace my singleness once again. It's been a blessing getting to know who I am as a woman. It's important to know the things you want and the things you need as a person. It's important to get healing so that you don't hurt others in return.

Today, I would consider my ex and I friends. We are able to be cordial with one another and offer each personal and professional advice. We are still very much supportive of one another and cheer each other on in our dreams and ambitions. Both desire the best for one another and wish each other well in all of our endeavors. We've forgiven each other and have both expressed the emotional, mental, and spiritual state we both were in during the unraveling of the relationship. That's a blessing in and of itself because I never thought

I would get to a place where I could see him or talk to him and feel good about it.

But now, in my wholeness, I can interact with him without any residue, pain, animosity or ill emotions. That truly is a blessing. I remember reaching out to him one time and saying I was thankful for everything we went through and glad that it happened. There are no regrets.

Y'all, I never had a major heartbreak before. I needed to go through that. I personally don't believe his intentions were to hurt me and I didn't intend for my verbal lash out to hurt him either. I believe we just thought because we loved each other, we would survive. How many of you know that if you don't have the right tools in your relationship kit, you're not going to survive. Doesn't matter how much "in love" you are or how much you go to "church." Doesn't matter how much you all "pray" together. Both of you have to get individual healing. Both parties need to be healed, whole, and secure.

Some of us in our religiosity would say, "God will never put his children through something like that. That was the devil! Why would he do you like that? Y'all was never supposed to get married! I wouldn't have married him. I wouldn't have married her. You made a mistake!"

Whatever your thoughts are, I can't change them. But, what I will say, and I'm not trying to be "religious," but it was good that I was afflicted. It was good that I went through that process. I have no regrets and no shame in saying it happened for a purpose. I will share that I learned so much about myself and I learned how to handle things the right way and regulate my emotions. I learned the power of not just communicating, but effectively expressing how I truly felt. I learned the true power of prayer and forgiveness. I also learned true fulfillment doesn't just come with a man, it comes in knowing who you are. See I thought after I got that word, that my ultimate fulfillment was having a husband. Y'all remember the word I got, right? Well, I had to learn that it was not all about just having a husband.

So why did I share this journey? Thanks for asking. I'll tell you why. My friends, the reality is at some point in your life, you are going to come face to face with the question, why me?

You might say, I pay my taxes, so why me? I've worked hard to get to where I am in life, so why me? I have good credit, so why me? I'm a law-abiding citizen, so why me? I don't smoke, drink, cheat or sleep around, so why me? I'm a lovable person, so why me? I am a good and faithful wife/husband or relationship partner, so why me? I give of my time and money freely to those are in need, so why me? I am a good father/mother to my children, so why me? I have a good personality and I am a people-person, so why me? I am a God-Fearing and praying person, so why me?

I don't know when it's going to occur, but the truth of the matter is, it's going to happen.

#AMOMENTWITHPRECIOUS

My brothers and sisters, please take note. Hanging on to guilt, shame, bitterness, anger, resentment, unforgiveness, embarrassment and insecurities is not the answer.

There are going to be some things that happen to you because of others; some things that happen to you because of your own choices; and some things that happen just because you are living. I know you've heard it before, but everything happens for a reason. Whether you like that phrase or not, it's just the reality folks. Everything in life has a purpose - the positives and the negatives. We must choose how to overcome when life doesn't go as planned. We have to learn how to get back up when life has hit you extremely hard.

So Precious, how do I turn my pity into purpose? I'm not going to tell you that your situation will turn out like mine or your process will look the same as mine. Every situation is unique and you need wisdom on how to get from where you are to where you want to be.

But what I will share is that you need a positive support system. Now, I am a firm believer in the Word of God and I can't force that to be your outlet but the Word, prayer, and my support system carried me. Find you a Word that's going to carry you. Find your place of peace. You have to find a way to get free from the weight of your past. We all need a release and we would be lying if we said we didn't. You deserve it.

~~~~~~

#AMOMENTWITHPRECIOUS

Forgive.

~~~~~~

I heard it said this way, "refusing to forgive someone is like drinking poison and waiting for the other person to die." Ask yourself, how long do you want to hold this over this person's head? When are you going to let go? Whoever it is. It can be a spouse, friend, parent, sibling, coworker, family member, etc. How long do you want to hold that grudge? Believe it or not, it's keeping you from moving forward. As I stated earlier, forgiving will not only set them free but, it will set you free all the more.

The road to wholeness isn't a popular road. Many choose to stay broken for a number of reasons that are beyond my control. I do know one thing, it's much better being whole than being broken. In the end, it's all about meaning and purpose!

My journey has been and will be filled with opportunities to be a blessing to myself and others (if it is the will of God). It only becomes about me when the chance comes for me to faithfully complete my mission (as it been revealed to me), and do so with a heart filled with gratitude.

~~~~~~~

#AMOMENTWITHPRECIOUS

When given the chance - be kind, patient, thoughtful, loving, grateful and always face the test or situation placed before you with the statement WHY NOT ME. Aim for the highest summit that you are able to fathom. Even if you don't reach it, you are still among the clouds and stars...not a bad place to be.

~~~~~~~

I'll conclude this journey with this. There is a story of a man who was lying on the ground by the pool who was in his condition for a long time. He was asked the question, "will you be made whole?"

I'll start by asking you this…How long have you been in your current condition. How long do you want to battle mentally, spiritually, and emotionally? How long do you want to stay stuck in the vicious cycle of heartache and pain? Unforgiveness? Bitterness? Emotional Trauma?

I'll leave you with the same question asked to the man at the pool. Will you be made whole? I don't care how long you have been in this state of brokenness, will you be made whole?

For me, I was in that condition for 5 years and I was ready to be made whole. Don't take as long as I did, be made whole now!

Shalom! (Nothing missing, nothing broken, nothing lacking, complete wholeness)

"When you start discovering who and what you are, it's bigger than anything you ever imagined yourself to be. And, by definition, it's generous. It's a generous exploration. The more of you you find, the more of you there is to give to those you love."

-Alan Arkin

I hope this book has encouraged you to realize there is a purpose for everything that we go through. It's up to us to turn the pity of why me into the purpose of why me? Understand, it's not so much about why you on the surface, rather, it's about the purpose of why you had to go through it.

Now it's your turn. Share your story!
TURN YOUR PITY INTO PURPOSE!

QUESTIONS TO PONDER:

1. What was your "why me" moment?

2. Who did you turn to when you were feeling lost and confused?

3. What did you do during this time to get answers to your questions? What was the outcome?

4. What purpose did you find in your pain?

5. What was your process in overcoming?

6. What did you learn from this book? How can you apply this to the process of renewal or becoming whole in your own life?

7. How did God reveal himself to you during your "why me" moment?

8. What did you learn about yourself?

9. How can you share your lessons learned and the process with others to help them?

10. If you didn't handle your "why me" correctly, what will you do differently?

11. What will you change?

How can I be substantial if I do not cast a shadow? I must have a dark side also if I am to be whole."

-C. G. Jung

Share your story
FROM PITY TO PURPOSE

In the pursuit of wholeness, there will surely be challenges but you need to keep going.

-Sunday Adelaja

How can one person love another if he or she doesn't know the person's history.

-TD Jakes

We must let go of the life we have planned so as to accept the one that is waiting for us.

-Joey Campbell

It is during our darkest moments that we must focus to see the light.

-Aristotle

What lies behind you and what lies in front of you, pales in comparison to what lies within you.

-Ralph W. Emerson

Your present circumstances don't determine where you can go; they merely determine where you start.

-Nido Qubein

Made in the USA
Columbia, SC
08 June 2018